the Black Rose

ALSO BY KRIS HAGGBLOM

Ghosts of Beautiful Women Dancing
Light Trace Glass Trap
Crossing Paradise
Inside the Wires
Dream Without a Dreamer
Consolation Prize
Chain of Silence
The Book Thief
Broken Time Machine
Exposure
Glints* (a chapbook series)
Solar Microscope
Solidago Wars
Twenty Flowers in the Ancient Manor
Features of Our Hacked Lagoon
Have You Preyed Today?
Seven Dragonflies I & II
No Song
Dawn of the New Age
Ghosts in the Wind

the Black Rose

Kris Haggblom

Poetic Justice Books
Port St. Lucie, Florida

©2019 Kris Haggblom

book design and layout: SpiNDec, Port Saint Lucie, FL
cover image: *Ghost Writing*, ©2018 Kris Haggblom

All rights reserved.

No part of this book may be used or reproduced in any manner whatsoever without written permission except in the case of brief quotations embodied in critical articles and reviews. Members of educational institutions and organizations wishing to photocopy any of the work for classroom use, or authors, artists and publishers who would like to obtain permission for any material in the work, should contact the publisher.

Published by Poetic Justice Books
Port Saint Lucie, Florida
www.poeticjusticebooks.com

ISBN: 978-1-950433-10-0

FIRST EDITION
10 9 8 7 6 5 4 3 2 1

for Dawn

contents

—	3
invitation	4
inquiry	5
interpret	6
harvest	7
who is my black rose	9
it fell to me	11
wipe	12
sand song	13
light fades	14
sunblind	15
who is my black rose	17
drowning	19
language has lost	20
secret	21
the phoenix	22
who is my black rose	25
inside the wires	27
grey magic	28
sleep	29
knife	30
another whisper	31
who is my black rose	33
the passage	35
walk	36
protest	37

grain by grain	38
arguing	39
who is my black rose	41
compass	43
luminous	44
sand	45
in the garden	46
o so black	47
who is my black rose	49
an image arrives	51
empty	52
trace	53
photgraph	54
exile	55
who is my black rose	57
black rose	59

the Black Rose

—

waiting for the ferryman
but Charon's gone fishing
I can hear him
whistling past the graveyard

invitation

at the curve
of her neck
breathe in
a whisper of
cloves and
wildflower tea
inhale desire
the soft down
of her cheek
sashays across
my lips

inquiry

yesterday and yesterday
reflections
dead reflections
that do not lead
to any meaning
to any tomorrows
why did you
have to go
why did you
have to
    go
how am I to fulfill
this inquiry
this today

interpret

walls cracked
pitted stone
a silent
forgotten language
awaken these memories
long and slow
long deep song
dream of sky
and trip the wind
interpret your silence
and rest

harvest

harvest of tears
caught before they
touch the earth
reflecting ghosts
casting memories
upon a pillow of winds
whispers racing
a howling loneliness
running through
fingers entwined
in lost prayer

Kris Haggblom

This silken haired, kohl-eyed gazelle that haunts these pages. Where has she risen from? A dark fire of lost desire smoldering in half-remembered dreams, she laughs as light as star dust reflected in moonlight. Lithesome and lean, she dances just beyond my grasp. The lure of the exotic has always pulled at the edge of reality. Surely this desert of words, tumbling from a star-filled sky and setting traps before our tongue was born of some enchantment. Whose? How did this sorceress discover my existence? Or, perhaps a better question, why haunt me?

Kris Haggblom

it fell to me

it fell to me
at the end of the road
it fell to me
at the end of the sky
the ocean caved in
and left a desolate
wandering behind
your eyes
the void
the zero
the abyss
the trembling of your lips
at the death of memory

wipe

lights play down the boulevard
comings and goings
memories and promises
she dances along the fountain
splashing her way to Paris
stars tangling in her hair and eyes
I trace the lines on a faded map
the crumbling architecture
wipes the sand from the table

sand song

the sand
sings
the sand
groans
the wind
buries
my howls

light fades

soft curve of
her silhouette
light fades
the stars
winking out
in her hair
the very stones
echo
desert's howl

sunblind

sunblind & breathless
I dream
in blue shadows
of blue shadows
fingers of magic
magic tracing
tracing magic
conjuring dreams
conjuring visions
grain by grain
building dreams
casting visions
casting dreams
incantations
cast to the wind
the grey wind
wind of the shadows
sunblind & deathless

Kris Hageblom

As I move through these dunes, strewn with wind worn stones, I realize that we do not choose our ghosts. Each stone represents a story from my past or future and each grain of sand between is each story's dream of itself. Is it even possible to determine which dream washed over by the infinite wind tumbled silently into my quest for recognition, for awareness?

Kris Haggblom

drowning

the swirling pools
of her eyes
push me down
drowning
the stars may sing the wind
yet that is not
where they come from
the roll of her hips
pulls the night down
I float into the sea

language has lost

language has lost
its anchor
now adrift
in a
meaningless sea
as the tight whorled
insinuations
work deeper and deeper
within my tongue's root
display insect cunning
a trap for unsuspecting
thoughts
stuck in the
mud at language's base
twist it off
and let meaning
grow anew

secret

the salty
spicy breath
a secret
drawn so deep
allow me to
lay here
forever
drown me
in the center
of your
universe

the phoenix

I knocked at the gate of night
and the stars let me in
their glittering ball
a palace of bright allure
we know why you're here
said al-'anqā'
twinkling in her skiff
join us in a draught and song
perhaps we may assist
but a ghost breath
may lead us astray

my kohl-eyed beauty
passed this way
sang I to the phoenix
you must know her well
all the heavens in her eyes
surely you've ridden
the dark waves of silk
black ripples in the wind
and the honey perfume
from the red clouds of
her lips and perfection
balanced twice and swings
low and soft within her hips
and arms to trap a soul

ah lovely indeed your dark eyed one
trilled the light as she passed
more evening wine
surely if she'd graced this place
bewitched as you we'd be
and al-'anqā' the phoenix star
moved closer yet to me
whispered hot and breathless
upon my cheek
perhaps *this* beauty will suffice
and rocked her hips
and my dreams of heaven's gate

and when I awoke
I held but a fistful
of sand

Kris Haggblom

But wait. Can't one recognize the spices stirred deeply into a well-constructed stew? Shouldn't I be able to perceive the ancestors of these visions? Soul piercing eyes and honeyed perfume do not arrive unaccompanied by some sort of baggage. But the tags are unreadable, piled with erasures and scraped and scratched beyond a useful language. Even the antecedents play with my mind.

Kris Haggblom

inside the wires

the music of communication
scored on wires
dances through our
inner cosmos
all played by
   Bullock's profound truth
on a crystal sphere
a demon goddess sips smoke
   casts dragons
carefully peeks through
an electric fence
the grid upon which
   we've hung our tomorrows
the lost words of Democritus echo
how do you bend
   the language of the stars?

grey magic

magic it's magic
blows away
incantations scribbled
in the sand
this world was never
far from falling
tripping or sliding
over its own edge
eyes that vanish
in grey winds
and whispers that
never betray

sleep

soft sliding sand
and swift tilt of stars
spin me back to ground
I close my eyes
to time's lullaby

knife

I burrow
make an indelicate incision
directly across her stomach
perfectly centered
between breasts and cunt
I slip in beneath her skin
inhale her
inside and surround
a red moist warmth
return to my mothery womb
I fall asleep in the delicious scent of our sex
sharp as a knife
light as the pillow

another whisper

desert of secret
ghosts scattered
like sand in hot wind
your breath
brushes the back of my hand
teases my ear
and falls away
before my eyes
may hold you

Kris Haggblom

I line up my suspects and then proceed to knock each one down. Playing dominoes with memories. The problem with my ghost game is that the players refuse to stay down. As each is removed from the list the previous suspects rise-up again, smile enigmatically and say, "Then again, it could be." But not one fits, really. And not a combination, either. My black rose is of a solid piece, not some assembly of best-remembered parts.

Kris Hageblom

the passage

if I sit
wait
by the water's edge
when I wait
at the water's edge
not long
not long
thirty years since
when I wait
sit
sit by the water's edge
I bow down
slide down
her beautiful rise
this moist flesh
damp hair
rises before me
this gorgeous
passage to forever

walk

red dress
silk
ripples in the wind
stars blaze
she laughs
a bit too loud
her head on my shoulder
we walk

protest

a bone jarring path
beneath a night sky
drawn down upon the earth
a blanket of fog
and the dust of dreams
connect the dots
my arm wraps loosely
about her waist
the fog of dreams
protests the dance of time

grain by grain

I lay out my desert
grain by grain
sun to sun
a lithesome dream
a tantalizing dance
at the edge of vision
vanishes
each grasp just beyond
the last grain
and so I begin again

arguing

existence stretches
a crepitation of joints
knocking
what's hiding outside that back door
knocking knocking
you gonna catch cancer from that
I don't think so
well 'thritis at least
it's always hard to argue with the dead
no matter how many times
I tell him he's wrong
we'll see we'll see

Kris Haggblom

Let me try a different approach. Why does my black rose present herself in a desert environment? I do not live in or even near a desert. Yes, I am familiar with deserts but it seems to me that she can appear nowhere else. Her dance through my vision is inextricably tied to the sand and sky of an unidentified desert. The Sahara, the Namib... Sonora, Rub al-Khali. Each echoes, none persist.

Kris Haggblom

compass

each morning
I begin anew
measuring the desert
she has presented
grain by grain
horizon to horizon
an endless compass
wielded by
a trembling hand

each night
her song
betrayed by the wind
and the arc of the stars
writes a new
dream of her eyes
displays the perfume
of my gazelle

she dances
with my soul
and I wake
and measure
my desert anew

luminous

luminous grey sky
luminous grey eyes
bent on dreaming
hypnotic swish
swish swish
fabric of dreams
swish swish
hips
breasts
swish swish
soft flowing
luminous

sand

we dip
slide
plunge
into the heart
of the world
it flows
through
our fingers
our hair
our teeth
explorer of our being
each multifaceted gem
clinging evidence
a slow flowing
living being
this
is what eats
everything
even the soul

in the garden

my mind flew off to her
her shadow in the sand
she appeared as a swarm
of blood red blossoms
nestled ominously
in a corner of the garden
the piercing perfume
and jangle of her bracelets
pull me down to
parted lips
a blurred memory
of long wet lashes
and lost whispers

the Black Rose

o so black

liquid eyes
and a burning moon
my gazelle has turned
a silken cheek
soft framed in black
o so black
the night may hide
in my gazelle's eyes
twine within the strands
that torture my sight
that nurture my dreams
o sorceress of the sand
lead me to the garden
a sip of sweet honey
a song to the wind
that would have me
die of thirst in the
arms of my gazelle

Kris Haggblom

Perhaps the key is time. One's ghosts need not be contemporaries. And, since she never speaks... others speak, but my black rose says nothing. She laughs; and it may be that I read more in her eyes, but what language is the language of stars and the motion of sand? These self-assembling visions of time flowing through her fingers... Do I envision these hands? They move smoothly, deftly tracing desire, weaving dune and wind in a ghost calligraphy that vanishes with the waking dream.

Kris Haggblom

an image arrives

an image arrives
unbidden
the conjurer of visions
settles
back
against
my soul
sings time
the sand
slides
silently
beneath my feet

empty

slip along the avenues
pursuing stars
that tangle in her hair
her eyes
her laughter
banging tumbling
down the alley
time lost
amongst the blowing sand
that seeps between the city's cracks

trace

this vision
these haunted
haunting eyes
did I even dream it
my hand
traces
this wind
sculpted
vision in the sand
the memory of
your smile
plays upon
my fingers

photograph

I think she
has walked away
left me to rot
alongside the dead river
I watch her fading
no looking back
dismissal tossed
over a painted shoulder
a pretty picture but
I don't even bother
to raise the camera

exile

I have wasted
a life
wandering these lands
of exile
and despair
a name
engraved
on my soul
washed in clouds
of sand
and the breath of stars
beckons
return
return
what may be
possible
those eyes
still burn

Kris Haggblom

This black rose, my gazelle, this representation of desire, of fitna*... a signifier of a post-language communication. Perhaps my kohl-eyed beauty is the telepathy of the stars, a love letter from the universe to a doomed race of demon dreamers; conquerors and slaves to their own fantasies marching to an all too obvious self-destruction.

Or maybe the vision itself is society's suicide note written in the sand and carried by the infinite wind to the distant edges of my mind. And so, back to the stars.

---

*the word *fitna* suggests something like 'charm, allure, enchantment, temptation, dissent, unrest, riot, rebellion' or all of these at the same time

Kris Haggblom

black rose

these are the rose sands
the rose sands of my gazelle
my gazelle's eyes
black as night
the sands that pass
with the rose winds
of my gazelle's breath
brush against my cheek
against my neck
black as night are the rose sands
soft as night on the rose sands
my gazelle has run as fast as night
though I still can feel
her breath upon my neck
return return
from your black sands
oh my gazelle
return

Kris Haggblom is a writer, photographer and bookstore owner on Florida's Treasure Coast. He has an AA from The College of Westchester, a BA from The University of Tampa, and a bs from life in general. He really didn't appreciate his stint in the Air Force. He still wonders why, if nature abhors a vacuum, we're all still standing here.

www.ingramcontent.com/pod-product-compliance
Lightning Source LLC
Chambersburg PA
CBHW030131100526
44591CB00009B/611